PRISONER ABOARD THE S.S. BEAGLE

Calvin Murry

ISBN 0-912678-53-4

Some of these poems have previously appeared in JOINT CONFERENCE, SEZ, THE PRISON WRITING REVIEW and the anthology from The Greenfield Review Press, THE LIGHT FROM ANOTHER COUNTRY.

Cover Drawing: "Crossing the equator on board the *Beagle*" by Augustus Earle.

Publication of this book has been made possible, in part, through grants from the National Endowment for the Arts and the New York State Council On The Arts.

Library Of Congress Cataloguing in Publication Data
Catalogue Card 83-81099
Murry, Calvin 1950- author PRISONER ABOARD THE S.S. BEAGLE
Greenfield Center, N.Y.: The Greenfield Review Press

FIRST EDITION

The Greenfield Review Press
Greenfield Center, N.Y. 12833

CONTENTS

THE WALLS

This is the mountain
peak of silence.
Isolate, in our eyes,
for here we scoop
time's glaciers.
Here we'd have you know
we're fine, we're fine.

Here we lie
lulled to perfection
guards who are grave images
clothed in a frozen hue.

Here we sleep
stomach to back, jammed
in one disguise:
tin sheets and corrosive groans—
ten cells each
with their own key
breathing when there's time
a growing fear of
the walls.

PRISONER ABOARD THE S.S. BEAGLE

There is, this moment, a man who knows
the gritty feel of things disturbed:
the murky flower tilted under
the full moon, the waxy drawl
of solitaire, and the stubble of bars
reflecting the cracked paint on walls.

He is loving his mattress so neatly pierced
with a finger. When he relaxes in the fog
that is prison, he smiles at me,
one con to another. It is this
peak edge that pulls
his shoulders down. The way he inhales

reefer and watches the pages turn
themselves—airbrushing the hidden strings
underneath Miss November's breasts,
or smooths his face with musk oil as he prepares
for nowhere. And it is this
moment that is pushing me, pushing . . .

Conjugal visits can distract a prisoner
but there is business at hand, for me,
in the shifting clouds above the fence,
where men no longer frequent beaches
with paper towels stuffed in their swim trunks,
where I am locked to the basin, its brassy eyes, coming

as they do in the rainfall of chaos,
resigned in the light that is with me.
I am thrust back in that cave
where the paintings are still livid, to amuse myself
near the stone footprints gutted
with dead leaves and discarded fruit, to see them

flare up into furrowed dreams
or into people as common as Amish grain,
or to run headlong to the sea of simple answers.
And if I could care, I would go to the desert
and give myself to the prickly pear,
for it carries its own water.

The prisoner with sharp utensils, who now
probes the walls, fashioning bodies
out of foam and paper plates, has snatched
out his eyes. I will offer my hand
and he will know it as braille, as I enter
the thick egg, and he will not care,
for it is when we don't care we are human:
We acknowledge each other with a glance.

THE LIFER

He isn't old except perhaps his fear.
All day he sits and sorts his shady past,
Whittling fragments from each year.
Alone, he carves and wears these silent masks.

He's doing time and differently,
attracting his keepers
like yellow to the night's deep glow,
while palming air
in the rut of his door.

Other convicts understand as well as I.
At least they know about the empty hands.
Though the man is sick, he makes good sense.
He isn't old except perhaps his fear.

Non ridere, non luger, neque detestari,
sed intelligere.
—Spinoza

7

HERMETIC VIEW OF DELUSION

He coughed
said it helps
clear air
of optics
folded his legs
into separate suitcases
or a secular chant

Imagine
he said
zazen
when bamboo burns
the feet of sleepwalkers
and the ash of empty sleeves rise
like the spires of a vacant motel
and accessible women are all fat or
worse
imagine them figments of captivity

WHEN THE MODEL PRISONER DECIDED HE WOULD END IT ALL

The bones are free, only this one,
this unbending, nerve-pinched con,
this lone columnar shadow
remains hung beneath the moon's deep glow.
The bones are breathing.
They are gone.
The face once so cool
lips fixed in a stitched smile
grins contented
grins at the absence of thought.
And nothing
not even the familiar fact
he is dead,
seems more a desertion
than his death.

So he gropes for nothing
smeared on the walls
in his mind.
and he falls into this state because
the noose around his neck is what matters.

IN

the shower
men obsessed
with 5 o'clock shadows
scrub all this away:

the rapists are pissing
in the washbasin
and burglars are screwing out
lightbulbs for their cells
the college kids are
smart
they have deciphered the drain pipes
and the old ones
are throwing soap
near their feet.

THE CHALLENGE

A hole in the right front pocket,
the shank nestling your leg.
You stabbed him so fast I fell silent
before the chow hall could breathe.
I couldn't see behind the shades of your eyes.
Had you known he was my friend
you wouldn't have done it, I know.
You'd have asked him, "How's the Mrs.?
    How you doing? Hope you get out soon . . ."
But something in your pocket obsessed you.
Your hands trembled at what he'd done.
You forgot, until a matter of conscience
opened the meeting as planned . . .

Later, we passed in the hall, the blood
on your face gone, the pants replaced
by gym trunks that exposed
your groin to the lights.
Dribbling the ball, you charged me,
eyes livid invitations,
as you challenged me one-on-one.

NEEDING YOU

For Michelle

When it rains I think of fighting.
When I get beat for a penny in the prison commissary
I think of fighting. I think of fighting when
incoming mail resembles the nose of Pinocchio.
I think of fighting when a guard says I can't kiss my wife.

When the sun shines, sometimes, I think of fighting.

               *   *   *

And when it rained, I cried.
I was fat as a ham,
a red bruise,
but your light struck me, quietly,
and out of this blue, sleep,
finally.

IN PRISON

A forked tongue flicks at sleep
Drags back earth to air

Eyes baseballs in a dirty mitt
Scratch the sunburn of nappy humburgs

Stylish brogues laid out for the big kill
Squeeze life out of thick mud, warmth out of day's end

Only night displays its shadow on crushed grass
Filled with pen-striped shells

Of discarded auto parts

Only trails in dust
Give away these secrets

That are waiting for a chance to spring

THE HARDEN CRIMINAL

Crazy stars swirling around touseled hair,
swirling in green soup,
swirling from the sink to the bunk,
and back again. Hands
that easily palmed a deck of
marked cards—empty now. Face
that could heat water
retracts its tentacles.
here mulls the prisoner
who is known by the puzzles in his pocket.
Light will enter his glazed eyes
no more, will bounce back
into its own answer.
Point at him and he will smile,

saying, I see so clearly!,

so that we wonder
if wind is rattling these windows,
or the sound of our breaths returning.

OF ALL THE THINGS YOU TOLD ME:

Suddenly, from the prison ceiling, the spider drops
      on a ninth leg of speech.
She tickles the underside of my belly and I take it
pincers are for touching. Promises ooze
from the stubbles of her skin. Her hourglass glows
in the dark, filled with bright
      engagement rings.
She threads a path in one ear and
out the other, and I smile, weakly,
listening to her breathing at a distance.

ON A SUMMER DAY, 1972

Precept, imperfect mudra
circling the mind like fear
over an Aztec altar.

I shield myself
as you bleed down the wall,
confinement your bright courage.

I think of you divine—
you died so young—
and I fear those deaths. The unknown,
the freedom you now know.

To touch fingers with cons *is* yours,
yes. And I tell you blood brothers are
in jails, as you bleed
so suddenly black.

now, the Bhagavad Gita and fire are mine.
The ritual this:
turn to the gasoline,
turn to the East, the rising
sun, turn to the wall.
And remember . . .

PRELUDE FOR A POET

The cathedral steps are burning,
there's no sudden prayer.
I give in and emperors uproot me.
I move back and forth in space,
in empty rooms, and the chatter
of powdered women at bridge games.
I attach myself to royal vestments.
I dance with Caligula in the parlor,
and grasp all rumors
in the fall of a cigarette ash.

Hopelessly entangled
I mount the guillotine,
and sit upon a certainty
that carries its own extreme.

PRESUMPTION

Did we actually stoop
in that fetal light
for those gutted cigarette butts,
inspecting them
like an old man inspecting toilet paper

And did we really surprise
those traffic cops
you commandeering the pedals
and I the steering wheel
How many trains
did we jump that year
How many books did we wedge
in those doors, our legs
sticking out like semaphores.

These are the moments
I bring you
coming as always on swollen feet,
my urine bag dangling
an attache case, and my face
a bruised, brown peach

SISYPHUS ANGERS THE GODS OF CONDESCENSION

I won't slide down that metal.
I won't slide down.
In the garden, beyond the shelter,
I refuse to leave, defend
against the kick.
And these wordless roses,
surrounded by dark trees,
throw up their dead.
The iron gods retract the spindled
sky from sight, shoulder it
past our open mouths.
And we choke on a personal silence.
In the garden—a breeze, chains rattle,
yet I won't go down this time.
My hands are made to grasp.

ASYLUM

I could spend my life
giving myself away.
I need the kind of woman who deserts me.
I am at my best in hotel rooms
where windows are boarded up and paint
flakes out in significant confusion.
I need the pearls of sweat
on my temples
after loving you at night. I need that drool
of blood and when you say those things
I smell the well-oiled engine outside.
Sailors collect darkness in duffle bags.
And a bruiser with "God" tattooed on his arm waits
for your return with my wallet.

FIX

A brother fans his voice at a speeding car
assuming the stance of some dead hero
bridging the canyon that halts all escape
and a glance that kisses the world's purse.

A voice under water makes bad girls blush
the only permissible supplication:
a man's voice on a thread of wind—and woman
shrugging off desire's tired needle.

ICONOCLAST IN THE BAR

"That's one thing I don't like, lice.
You take a piece of that urinal soap,
put it in your ass pocket,
and the lice'll leave you."

He's ripping beer cans and pretzels with bare hands.
Outside, the moon points out fake jewels and slow
cigarettes. Inside, buried on a sofa with broken springs,
he drums out a message for the music of his mind.

The sober slap of brine and cigar picks out faces
in this shadowy place, pitched in a dream, and lights
laughter in women with cut-glass rings.
He hampers their progress with shards of protest
as cops toss him out into the street again.

PHYSICIST IN THE BATHROOM

He is polishing figurines in the bathroom.
Lyrics echo off the tiles.
He knows he will be saved in the end.
He has been there so long the pin-ups are yellowed
from the mornings of shaving cream and steam.
The insurance men hate that kind of longevity,
but he goes no farther
than the assembly line, or
escapes in the dark room
with a copy of *Hustler.*
so what if a graduate hangs in the crapper all day,
while polishing glass and improving the feel
of suppliant girls success can buy.
Changes here are relative.
Once, out of wedlock, he created a child,
and the child filled out,

20

ponderous, and his wife,
who wore noxema, changed,
could not be dealt with,
Things, she yawned, change.
But that was long ago . . .
Now, he sings to the tiles,
and writes anonymous letters
to the born-again voyeur, and lectures
on the poverty of the nucleous.
And beyond a dullness of the aperture,
there is a mating of the eye—the lens,
the woman and child, swelling
larger than life.

REFLECTION OF THE WEALTHY BANKER STROLLING IN SHELBY FOREST

Aiming to miss the sidewalk cracks
you stumble past a life of lights
you enter a forest of hands
an obedient forest of old
trees, acceptable substance
for being with.

Now you are upside down and the trees
stack themselves into black boats.
You can't recall the last time
all that was green settled in ripples
ahead of you. Nor the time
your inner tube sank
on a glass lake

and you counted your riddled lives
again, again, and again.

WHEN DOING TIME AND
ALL ELSE IS WRITTEN

I.
was not for me to feel . . .
handcuffs dead barracudas, teeth
stabbed tight, diminished flesh . . .

was not for me to think—
but had I thought
I would have been aware: the breathing,
the lips, and the
prodigal blood . . .
returning to know me.

was not for me to feel . . . to feel . . .
legs stirring, now stalagmites,
and stirring,
restrained by walls: geometric
isolation. The mind is elsewhere, commuting
with alien images.

II.
I remember. It was mentioned
in passing, the death,
the muscle and matter and granite:
the petrified condemnation someone spoke of,
the coolness,

the civilized lama—some urban Himalaya . . .
veinless hands welded to the groin.

and I see myself beyond
the aperture of distance. Spread-eagle
and darting, arms towed by current.
Now I am swimming . . . and feeling . . .

I am swimming like polluted fish and floating,
buoyed in the gentle sloop of your eyelash.

I see myself beyond
imagistic sunrise

22

JAZZED OUT

If I bubble twice and rise
to the surface
someone scrapes my head.
If I hear the constant sound
of the universe
it is aluminum beer cans
and Coltrane.

2 things I remember:
  Diaphanous silence of Ionesco
  and my hand shaking hands with my hand.

IN THE KYOTO GARDEN
THE MONK IS STROLLING

Unfolding, this old man is the landmark.
A warmth touches the backs of his knees,
as white foam trails from each thought.

He moves on.

At the porch
of the polished stone
he slips through the stems
of his cupped hands.
His lips form the question

and the silence gives up its petals.

THE SEEKER'S ANNUAL VISIT HOME

I'm here to show you how fat I've grown,
how my muscles sag, and how, near evening's
end, I turn pale green in the pull
                    from your strange blood.

I've come this far to tell you the flame
from the kerosene stove is its own reason.
Even air turns a different shade.
Yet, I know the hang-out of the well-wrought sage
and the reverent space of the fleshy crow's feet.
I know the concubines of bas relief
who preserve the sacred seed.
I know the high one who's beside himself
                    on the headless mountain.

Now, I'll crack the Tibetan Book
passed from hand to hand.
I'll ask for my birth papers,
and deny them, as I search
their byline for the synonym of pain.

I've studied the axis of origination.
Is this my mom? Black hole
of her squinting eyes sucking in
the world? Is this fragment the relic
of a once warm circle I struck out
from, seeking chilled breasts?
Is this the chart of swells
and uncertain descent? The ache of her rocking
chair a vacant proposition.

Is this her position? . . .

This much I accept: the faces of strangers
in subway windows are the same as her face.
A polished jewel is its own refracted light,
an abstraction full of grey speech.

I stare at her greying face.

24

The thought that led me here,
through arcades and narrowing ashrams,
has left me, deposited on this doorstep,
where this face gazes
from the bedroom window at hubcaps. They are
transparent, their answers cataracts in her
unassuming eyes, as she nods to me, touches my wrist,
as one would a visitor, or a guest.

MITOCHONDRIA

And in 1959 I took a trip
to Europe, raced with Hitler
for the Holy Grail. I found his legend,
in black, on its fly page. I found
his heart, in black, in Poland.
I scaled the cliffs of Longinus
on hands and knees, a monkey
on the barbed point of death.
Egypt had no knowledge of its own
erections, had no measure of the numbers
wrapped in plain brown skins.
It was here I chased Napoleon
into the bedroom of answers, and emerged
pale as canvas, a somehow different man.
I sipped tea on Fuji with Li Po
(having learned the proper pinky
from Confucius in Da Nang.)
Samurai women did well without armor,
and their men could sing.
England caught a flash that saved their day,
while their Orders of the Dawn
sat vomiting on the floors.
This too was the day
Nostradamus knocked,
and the day the Kybalion blew in.

In Little Rock I courted
the mother of Glut—foodstamps hidden
in her pantry drawers, a pricky
little finger clutching madly at her blouse,
while in Memphis black Spinozas
were quietly keeping house.

This is the room I come to when I'm not
on the go. These my texts, my potato plant,
my stipends, my truss, my kitchen,
my puja rack, and in my wallet a picture
of job, next to a dollar for the bus.

LOVE MAKING

War stifles our brightest invention.
We couldn't cough under God's great snow.
We couldn't breathe while the lives of others
were still beneath the storm
of our worst intention. We
could but taste the blood that covered us,
that sprouted trousers of its own.

When the guns are silenced, we've nothing
to do, so we turn to our navels,
or the young girl who thinks too much.
We struggle through countless tv dinners
looking for iron, and the message
in Irish potatoes. We argue in the market,
Arabs of discontent, savoring the women
who are masters of this earth.
They don't know us.
In peace, they don't care.
In peace there is dandruff to be washed from their hair.

The fighting stopped in December. We the survivors
stood on a mountain, surveyed our latest loss.
We tenderly pointed to our groins: a future
of prosperity, we found, had died. The victors
wanted more, from this wasteland of minerals.
They wanted our leader, and our treasurer of precious jewels.
And we cried. They wanted none of us,
none of us at all.

When the guns are silenced, we're without reason.
We sleep, dreaming of the woman who forged the key
to our closet of futility. We storm garbage cans
on our quest for meat. We're the boss of nothing
these women don't own.
They want none of us.
They now demand the millionaire—
and none of us at all. They forget
we fight because we're built for it—
not because we desire it.
We make our own battles when nothing else will do
We're being diminished, and we may lose!

So here's the plan to save us all. Give up
a part of earth to the God of mountaintops.
We've come down, the women know it.
The millionaire was captured years ago, and we
are sole proprietors of the mountains and the deserts.
Our promises are more than flakes from a throat. They're
promises from slaves with none to fight for.

We're dogs in a petshop, waiting to be picked
as nature's cruelest failure and the world's
      first trick.

CERTAINTY

I stake my life on every lover I've had.
I put my chips on feelings I know, and that's why
I'm frugal as hell.
Women don't know what they're getting.
I'm a gift.
Every relationship falls at my end.
I have aces up my sleeve for tight situations.
I'll come out on top with most any woman—
and every woman if the kitty's small.
30 years experience is enough I'd say.
In me the scars of backrooms and adulteries which're
succinctly and invariably mine.
I'm the kind of guy who doesn't bluff easily, and bartenders
like that.
I'm casual but dominant.
Somewhere women are dreaming only of me.
I know. I feel it right about here.

MACHISMO

A pimple appears at the edge of my smile
I look in the mirror and beyond that
the running of the bulls, the workout
at Joe's Gym, the X-shaped virgin
on a cool sheet, and beyond that another
virgin, like rabbit-ear antenna
on my James Bond VCR recorder.
And above me another mirror
supported by three big balls
and the multiplying virgins of the satin space.

So this pendulous pimple I squeeze
into place— like this.
Now I'm another posture.

I raise my left leg and I'm
a Greek statue in perpetual
flight, a glistening gladiator
at Madison Square Garden.
Anything contained in a hand-held
mirror is mine.

But a full length instrument is another matter.

CATHOUSE LOVE

In the morning, sitting on edge, as always,
you remember most the stain, a slightly smaller
stain, a little less visible stain, than the one
you imagined. Something of you lost among floral disaster,
Chivas Regal balanced on the breath, a stem of grass
rooted in the nostril's yawn, these are given,—no taken,—
to the furry fever of the brain, and that distant spot—
a different body, above her stretch-marked abduction. . . .
In the haze, the body forgets, spills out
into dawn. But you remember, yes you, one wet, sorry kiss,
second-hand human flowing into fright, and your footsteps,
after you, at a muddy-brown stuttering trot.

BLACK DOG

Having endured the flat breasts of an old woman
I know why numbers are in elevators.
I can imagine servitude in Bangladesh.
I could own up to the centerfolds in my wallet.
I could eat fish raw if picked of bones.
Tonight, I dream of a lazy dog
that sleeps on my thigh, asking nothing.
I will call it Rover.
I will feed it cake.
In the morning, I'll grease my kinks
and visit a European bar, drink
with the German who knows the value of color.
When the last light is lowered, and again
I'm alone, there will always be that terminal,
that ageless woman, waiting.
She too has a reason for wearing white,
and for that black dog howling
    at moonlight.

PHYSICAL THERAPY

I was attacked by many things that night.
I was attacked by the woman who lives above me,
but who never hears me, and by the friend I feared
for being too much friend, and the landlord
who repeatedly asks me my name.
I was attacked by bartenders serving happy hours
at closing time, when Detroit was most itself.
I was attacked by the dope that made me dream
of the cumbersome van, its steering wheel purring
under my lover's hands, circling Missouri, and me.

I was cold that night, the night you talked too much,
the night you pressed your face into the wind,
turning into someone I've never known. I never

loved you, and you never meant to hold me that close.
You never thought your mom's well would run dry,
and that we'd search each other's eyes for water.
You never thought we'd go that far, on a tank of gas,
on a lot of words, on each other's nerves. My own

dear love— I loved you not. . . .

I was attacked by many things that night.
I was sitting on the floor, nursing my back,
when I noticed you drawing up, a treacherous spasm
of the shoulder, so I sipped a beer, easing
the pressure. A criminal I'd known for years
walked me through the red-light district of Highland Park,
down a nameless street. Only then did I suffer
the ambivalent shoulder. I felt I'd die on this street.
I grew sick of incense that burns too quick,
leaving me helpless in the face of clear thought.
Dogs in every alley panted for me under my window.
That night the moon cupped a whore's breast,
and lightbulbs didn't burn as promised. I felt alone,
imprisoned in this cheap room that stank
of orgies, impervious dreams, deadly drink. I poured

myself into its silence, pounded my chest for life.
I called a god whose answering service only opened garage doors.
I turned to the walls and it was there, these things
on a wall, in fine print, meaning what every hobo meant.
I saw myself a victim. I could no longer fight.
I was attacked, enslaved, by my lover's voice—
    and by guillotines serving up night.

EACH MORNING WHEN
YOU LEAVE FOR WORK

It happens with unerring dependence.
I can't forget your name.
Heaviness?
    And the dirty carpet that sticks to feet.

Silence sits beside me
like thick blood.
Flecks of black at each elbow
remind me of hot tar.
Outside, footprints of thin
children circle edges
of grassy fields,
your face, spindled on the pillow,
faces west.

You will not move
if I touch you. You are gone
in an instant—last week's news
in the wheels of a Ferrari . . .

Did you think me easy
to escape?
Duty?
    I will catch you by degrees.
    I will catch you by degrees.

NODDING OFF

I crane my ear to the pin prick
kids rush out from the last day of school
and into this dark arcade, down these arteries
of empty ghettos and autumn blondes, down,
farther still, to the light flicker of my balls,
colored by that surprising blush on my wife's neck.

She is not my wife. Gravity owns her.
Nor these kids, their faces the trademark of heroin.
Balloons inhabit this body in knots, drunk
as junkies. They are multi-colored and carry their own
    strings.

DREAM BAIT

Snapping awake I strain
to get back to that place
where I am somebody else.
Where the stretch of thin arms
almost touch my eyelids.

As I often stretch
my own thin arms
to touch you, at night,
in a half-forgotten past-time
of a half-hypnotic command.

Only to find you
by the window, sipping coffee,
feeding my wallet to piranhas.

RAIN AT THE DOOR
OF THE BASEMENT APARTMENT

Rain slanting through tight windows & doors,
Life filters in broken patterns:

The wino shakes food from the bottle tip
And swallows spit.

The kid confined to one foot of backyard
Searches for the fourth wheel of his wagon.

(Time continues,
The hub of all traffic.)

The mother blinded by closed drapes
Forgets to shut the dishwasher door

Though a captured bird beats
Wings against a revolving floor.

Below the street long lines of women
Claim unemployment fees for epilepsy.

And those who past them are never certain
If they point to small black rooms,

Or new roads to sharp diversions.

CONSENTING ADULTS

Tonight, I'm sipping beer in an empty pasture
and someone's approaching.
Two Cardinals in a leafless tree
take turns haggling
over the greyness of worms.
They're bitching over vandals in their nest.

They're in that fork of diverging limbs,
where beaks excuse the forest
where no farmer works.
The air's sharp now,
my fingers can't grasp the bottle neck.
I've much to be thankful for,
especially you, especially you
shuddering my letters back.

LOGIC

I have a reason. Madness does have limits.
A thin line links us to a common dream. You are
Napoleon; I named you that, for the blood tooth
God gave me to give you. Napoleon,
conqueror of mystic chateaus, hieroglyphs, people
you'd like to know, or have known, dreams
that return to that one place, each time, a spike
hurled from war's heaven, jacketed in light.

I even named light. Called it God. Held it
to night's spooky branches and perceived
filthy conjectures on every billboard sign,
and girls who spell my relief for a dime,
and urine stains on the porches of tenements
all bearing Catholic names. I grew up
on the second flat of St. Dominic. Met girls there,
painted women who look like someone
I should've known— with their smells of mattresses,
picked over chicken, and conspicuous spots of baby piss.
In the alley, behind the gym, St. Ladislaus pukes up
another dead. I could picture the whiskey truck
that usually burst their heads. Then I heard
the cattle truck making its rounds
in the dusky silage of this northern town—I knew
who this man might be, ole Henry himself,
laid low by a trumpet, or a dream.

CPR

You got nothing, absurd mother,
with your dry ass against dry concrete.
Nothing, brother, that the maid doesn't own,
your crabby hands locked to your saggy thighs.
You got nothing that the mayor didn't promise

on his way to Bangladesh. You saw only
the flicker of his saraband, the starched finger
of an insinuation. Did you know that?
Repulsive trick, staring at tires on ambulances,
pitching a bitch, you haven't got shit—
and she told you that while she skimmed up
her rags and split. Your ace confessed
to a social disease, and your car broke down
at an all night hamburger joint.
You didn't have a dime for the jukebox.
You ate crackers, and you dreamed of the waitress
who lives in California, scented in lotus.
The one who nods into a pink champale.

No trains stop at this hotel, with its windows
seeping secrets from each crack, and the radiator
smells of abused, aborted babies. . . .
No Wall Street Journals ring doorbells here,
no mailman has extra samples of Rolaids.
Just you, here, up to your neck, strangled
by a love you couldn't explain, despite clever ways.
Here, nature's own reply, in your best bathrobe,
in your cleanest stocking feet, because you couldn't
touch the small of your woman's back, couldn't twist
the stupefying crack about her breasts
from your mouth. You lost out
to the minor who sells foodstamps, and stinks
of a wet dollar. You haven't got a chance,
and I hurt to tell you that: I too
have slept in bus stations chainsmoking
cigarettes, rapping to the girls of Canada,
and dodging management threats. I too have heard
The Delta Blues down in Mississippi.
And I too have brushed away the dirt from a discarded burger.
I can tell you of the tainted onion.
I can point you to the whore who drinks Magnum Beer.
Don't tell me of your dying aunt, and your babies
dreaming of milk. Don't please, spill
your best lies on me. Rise above
this shit, man, and *Breathe.*

SOLDIER OF FORTUNE
RETURNS UNNOTICED

If I blink the spell is broken,
the mass of greed cracked by a thunderbolt,
the logic of movement strapped to an oak,
the electric whine of a bad garbage can,
the haggard advance of a neutered pet. . . .

I push myself through quicksand and ice.
I lower my eyes among autumn leaves.
My Congressional Badge of Honor tarnishes
      my teeth. So I aim at these:
a twist in rational order, like some syllable
or serial number, or the riddled dog tags
      of an objective. 00000, how I'm struck

by that cortex of resemblance, garnishing
the number on my neck. It is not Pythagorean.
Man and nature miraculously combined not
by G.E., or Westinghouse, or nondescript
drugstores and dusty showers. But by me.

Destruction buzzes over Old Ben. I kiss my wife
without blinking. I make love during
Dallas and Green Bay. Halftime 1968. A starched
fog settles in my left breast pocket,
in my secret napalmy smoke. But the enemy
is gone, and the face flies off
among the foliage. No one greets me
as I step from the plane, no locks are left
      unchanged. . . . .

              *   *   *   *   *

This prison has stood for so long one might think it was
     conceived by God
in a purple moment of boredom, when the wind swirled
     aimlessly
through fingertips of speculation, and man
designed his own birth. In prison we're similar,
apportioned one corner of this wide world. Nameless,
we need no reason to communicate what's given wardens.
And the spiral of the brain needs no sight beyond these walls . . . .

                    *   *   *   *   *

Sunlight bounce
like compasses broken. Oranges,
peaches, pears, wooden steeples
beyond reach.
Grubby knuckles shade the face from engine burns.
Morning fades into a black gown discarded.

          "All soldiers are liars,"
          the solider said.
          Liars, liars indeed . . .

               *   *   *   *   *

No one greets me as I disembark,
quietly nibbling a salmon sandwich,
stroking a footpath on a concrete floor,
similar to the horror of an unopened door.
I shut my eyes and all scars disappear.
Soap dice harden in a service station john.
All that remains is this Purple Heart,
ceramic amnesia and a mosquito screen;
all I know is that I drowned in the stillness of the world's
     brown face,
silently picking a sun-bleached bone,
and rattling the doors of somebody else's
     locked home.

COERCION

I'm hating you it's as simple as that
sitting here on the flecked breast
of the world on the ledge of the window looking
down chain smoking and each
red spark a picture of you

approaching and the enemy is less
defined in the brake lights and spinning
wheels screaming to a stop
I refuse to consider anything other
than total amnesty a studded condom

a wallet-size copy of the autobiography
of Idi Amin and a rabid rat
for we have come this far
on such things fucking in the birdbath
at city hall or sharing the ceremonial

wine of the oppressed persona for we are agreed
that we love the oppression of the other and we know
the call of the vulture nibbling our flesh
our extended fingers we know it is traitorous
to appreciate the bareness of bones

which is all you've taught me of the sight
and alignment of the trigger housing and the squeeze
and I'm hating you it's as simple as that
while firing round after round saying
to the black birds circling my mind

how quick we take flight
upon the merest mention of humanity

and how I'm hating the thought of you

THE EXPATRIATE ARTIST DECLARES FRIENDS TO BE

Lights flicker on a distant hill,
    Faces as faces in the heart-strap's thump
Motionless, leaning, mouth filled
    with surprise shaped by a patient skill.

Far beyond the knife-edged hump
    the weight of these shadows stand.
Logic laughs, the wristwatch stops,
    suspended from the arm of an oak-like stump.

Night won't touch my potted hands.
    nor the upward thrust of vampire bats.
The shrill confusion of a dry creek bed
    Is the sound of the sun on old beer cans.

Standing diminishes my island, but less
    Than the dragging footprint of sweat.
With my eyes to the earth-swell of this salty crest,
    I strain to populate with a cigarette.

OCCUPANT AS HERO OF TIMES TO COME

Gone are the no-more ideologists of america.
Gone are the systematic rhetoricians
of the safe and simple dream.
Gone the shocking black fist of another generation.
Gone the norman mailer specifics of genetalia and generals.

Gone are they all, to the platitudes of inaction,
the black lace of fear.

Organic functions mushroom into holocaust.
Hands return to the politburo of selfishness.
Soul on Ice discussed and dismissed by ladies of the night.

Gone the kilroys of suburbia, mom's apple pie.
Gone the marx brothers and their secret word.
Gone, too, the belief in the grace of God.

Gone are they all, to the platitudes of inaction,
the black lace of fear.

And where have all the flowers gone?
Certainly not to the black grave of the black king.
Nor to the pat boone of white lies, the diplomat of August.

Somehow the head still moves, but its thrust
is aligned with the pelvis,
with the goddess of negation,
and the mailbox opening to a monstrous bed:

When junkmail diminishes, the occupant's dead.

NOTHING PERSONAL

I've no degrees in this life
I'm empty of ecumencial pain

I sleep in the Club of Shifting Eyes
I eat whenever I can.

I'm fond of ugly women
thus I wear rejection well.

I refuse to read the Book of Job
as I'm often objective as hell.

I write what I want if feeling good
though I suffer from bloody piss.

I'm known at the House of the Leperhood
as one who tips with a kiss.

NEUTRALIZING THE RADICAL ELEMENT

I sit on the staircase of the psycho ward
listening to current of solid gowns
                    and threadbare slippers
                    and scattered testicles
daring sunlight at the back of nothingness
daring nothing that runs down halls
daring radiators of secret signs to blind me

The headshrink is leaning on a waterfountain
drinking linguistics, twisting his smock
                    in the dusk of subtle innuendos
saying something
                    about my uncomfortable hair
                    about kneading the edges of my eyelids
                    into perpetual surprise

I say nothing
                    pretending confusion
I point toward the fall of seagulls
                    in the arms of an angry Atlantic

CHILD SUPPORT

The simple things frightening by degrees:
sleeping under the sky, reading
discarded newspapers, stealing
a drink from a waterhose,
and chasing . . .

Not easy to fool, I've been around.
I remember the windbreaker
she burped on, while you and he
lit silence in the next room.

Woman, I know
without moving my lips,
only easing the burden
to the scotch and sports page.
Woman, you said she's mine. I'm

not easy to fool.
Here's an intensity I've yet
to show you. The hands do have
a purpose for the beer can,
the sifting through leaves for the footprint.

And there're things to be said
for air and shirt sleeves.
And for what I give in an instant.

Woman, did I do it right?
The routine accessible
even to this distant catcall?

Now, in the place you once were,
reading the soap rings *she* left
in the bathtub, I'm frightened
by shaving cream and shot glasses,
the chewed end of cigars:

Those simple things, not his, but *mine.*

INVASION OF PRIVACY

Waiting in the silent shower,
waiting for the terrible cleansing,
the spray with its mind of winter,
self-fulfilling like the force of
    time. In an hour

she must march toward that brassy nozzle.
She must choose without rush, all showers
    cold and identical.

She stands before the steel door, fogged
in a watery light,
before deciding one quick dose is
better than one slow drag.
And she swells suddenly, casting up
    disgust, falling
beneath the grey pierce.

In the morning, executioners will glance
at her body, the rigid nipples,
buttocks of concrete.
They will avoid her stuck vision,
her big-nose discontent.
Avoid the whirls of water where her flesh
    won't sink.

And they will dream of the man and women
whose thighs revealed no easy answers.

EXILE

Nothing fantastic
but the dream
in the corner
the black grip of bars
on walls

Letters on the
bedside table
ornately spiced
neatly typed
perfumed
perhaps the tip of a mind

                          (insert): Kafka, Franz

Cigarette holes in grey trousers
fragments of poems
of movement around the lips
the well-timed entrance of
Eliot, Crane, Pound

                          (insert): Kafka, Franz

Nothing else
only the window
admits distractions:
the prison factory
the full moon
perhaps the sweet
smell of a jackal's womb

                      (insert): Kafka, Franz

A MAN'S FAULT

How quick it skips out   ·
on the lake's lid of clear thought
and constant angles of something said
in the stop-pulse of the breath's
holding back, heaving nothing.
My aim has been to please you
in as many ways I can remember
the names of our neighbor's children.
There are holes in my t-shirt
speaking to this, clinging to the light,
in which we both grew bold in shadows
of kindled flesh. New births
are everywhere—like roots
on old trees, landslides like
small shoes up man-made hillls.
How nice we return to this, admonishing
the kids we didn't bring; saying their parents,
too, should be more considerate,
as we, drawing apart, toss stones
across surface refractions,
forgiving ourselves, then each other,
our most childish actions.

AUTO-EROTIC WARD B

He has only OM to say.
That's not enough. He waits
for the studded strap,
the paper cup, the friend
who doesn't come. And waits,

his hand hanging
like a disconnected phone.
He smiles at the plant
that spins the chamber
in his head. The faceless
attendant loads another
paper cup. Too late,
my God, too late.
A brother has finally jumped.

ON THE MASON-DIXIE LINE
AS I CONTEMPLATE DIVORCE

I enter the world alone and I get out of it alone.
This grey earth, around me, whispers repeatedly
as I might whisper through the sleeves of green trees
at each intersection.

Now the slumped sky moves as a man from his wife.

Averted eyes, curbed by rapid suspicion, dot
these thin lines into night. You and I,
backs to the wind, lean horizontal through another state.

I remember only the hands, your hands, and that sea-shell
     phone . . .

Nothing startles me, now, not even your mom's monotone.

POEM TO A RELIGIOUS PRISONER
WHO IS NOW
AT CENTRAL STATE

Sitting coolly on the windowsill
of his forehead
digging in for the first
among many waves of attack
the hunted remains the hunted.

It is written that salvation comes
riding micro-waves
bandaging believers in flaming folds
the soul squeezed from the nostrils like toothpaste
tears like wine and wilted roses
in hospital rooms.

O victim of existence
the truth shall set you free.

Eating from tiny paper plates
thanking God with abundance
he declares to no one particular
that he will eat only
the little people of his karma
and proceeded
to eat the leg of his cellmate.

O victim of existence
the truth shall set you free.

SNEAK PREVIEW

Lying there, predators of the unsuspecting,
glazed eyes above a cover of dirt,
waiting for the brief heartbeat, thinking who
among us God chooses to alert
this moment's stalk, this mind's tease.

Hands at the ready, cradling tired skulls,
yet quick as a trigger at the sound of the first born's voice,
hot to trot, ready at a glance to pounce
on command, to engage the obsessive question,
to count up the wet truths released on a prison floor.

Just lying there, eager as a junkie's needle
and sick of the TONIGHT SHOWS, the late night soaps,
now dog-eared from the breath's molestation.
And the breath, held in abeyance with anticipation,
that comes—from the bowels—a near-growl:

> *Shot, Shot!* Our pointman screams. We
> are all eyes, penetrating glass and plastic.
> *We're looking at this woman's thighs* . . .
> We're trying to see if Nietsche is right,
> that the same sun rises at the South Pole
> We're trying to crack prison's ice,
> get something flowing . . . .

And will she understand this vital greed
caked upon our backs by the pressure of cages?
Will she understand the chains binding our every year
to yesterday's death of our closest kin?
Will she open up our other eye, in our tense sleep,
sensitive even to air, in this garden of adrenalin,
    in these quicksand shoes of despair?

A prisoner never knows what's in the world.
He knows only how quick this piece is snatched away.
Lying there, poised
in utter disgust at the rude break
of encroaching day.

ATTICA EQUATED

You wake to nightmare feet
Soldiers with skullcaps that whistle
Soldiers who march to your cell, and straight
To your bunk   They tuck you in a Jew's body
Chain your Japanese hands
To your African ass
Drive stakes into your Russian feet
And their gun butt gags your scream
Only your toenails has a thick enough flesh
To stick out from under blankets
Your head a wish these lichens of fire
Will die   You've heard about others who fell
The boat-people the prisoners
The iconoclasts of both terrible letters and love
The Sargasso Sea the janitor with your hair
And the rabid minister of filthy air
When the dust settles on your diminished wake
You still smell those friends you knew by name:
    Fidelman Kenyatta Cochise

A gun butt's drowned your scream.

POW

Do you want me to grin back in your face,
whack your back with a hearty cheer?
Desolation and death have mortared this place
with the blood of prisoners no longer here.
Do you want me to kiss your feet,
pay homage to this your finest hour?
I, for one, have no need to appease
your servants of iron and ungodly power.
I make no claim to immortality.
Like you, I seek small, earthly breaths,
I know well who I shall be—
this I'll argue facing even death.
If you must confront my unflinching stand,
go ahead, kill, but I shall die a man.

PAPIMANES

I asked the Roshi to explain his paddle.
No answer is in his wrinkled hands,
no rustle distress his robe.

He knows no one. The sound
of his sandals echo only the forest,
the silence of his chant
a leaf around his head.

Perhaps he *is* the answer, of coming and going,
a sun-raft beyond any chaos,
a nourishing thought in a bowl of green tea.

But ask the question
and he'll laugh and say, "Ah."
Ask again he'll slap his knee and grin.

Little is given the students who enter
squeezing their nuts in their beggar's bowls,
stripping their body to the night's inquisition,
detached from the disciplined darkening of seasons.
Little is given, but the clap of the gong,
and the shuffle of flesh on stone.

         *   *   *   *   *

In frightening summer the fruit flies' gossamer
crash among broken branches and bones.
We sing to walls and a moss-fed creek, craning
to pricks and distant replies
of the fruit picker's hands that are prodigal sons.
We dream of rana meat, and the horseman who passes
factories and skinned goats and whispering seas,
    whispering *o philosophers, o worms* . . .

         *   *   *   *   *

While light echoed across the sphere
of my head, having rippled
over the lines of my legs,
I was Kudzu on a thousand roads.
The smell of milkweed was the smell of peace,
as I charged senoritas in Spain
and the brawn of stampedeing bulls.

Then I heard the bright chant of shores,
the spiral of incense on cliffs.
I heard the frayed koan known only by the Roshi
in the synaptic nod of his dawn:

    Suzuki changing diapers, watching
    the diaper flowing around rivulets
    of flesh, grasping the girth
    of innocence. The child
    Suzuki, palmed in a mudra—
    sound and flesh in a bamboo mold.

Perhaps this is the lesson I learned from that man.
Or this I know of Rinzai Zen:
    What, I ask, is the purpose of your paddle? . . .
The Roshi only grins . . . .

BLOOD BANK

Something's not right, that he should be a bum.
Not right that he should give his best secrets
to the wind, his finest instances smutted out
by a reefer-riddled thumb.
Not right that he should hug his days in the pocket
of his ill-fitting coat, though parked outside
hums his grandest ways: finding a place to dump the nights.

He doesn't care, so he pulls his drawers
from the grip of his days, and with the firmness
of a drunk, he pounds down the stairs.

(Not right that he should be the bridegroom
to what the saddest of us see, as we descend
our own stairs on a silent ghetto street.)

I smoke too much to say specifically
Melville was right about the fast food chains,
and the great white whale, and the rum.
I'm too dazed by the woman who talks too much
and never removes her shades.
The bottom line is that I don't know
what the next child will be:
there's too much on the print-out.
Too many attorneys.
No one bakes bread anymore.
And sharks inhabit the sea.

I wouldn't dare address such a man as he,
stumbling into his vehicle, his great white sprint,
speeding down our busiest alley
and into the center of our wonderment

SOCIAL SECURITY

Flesh turns a rancid brown on any summer evening,
swells above the brainstem, throbs through the history of birth.
A soldier warned us of the riverbed, and we counted our change
while descending the subway, sampling the dust between
  railroad tracks.

Quite a while now, the day we laughed,
then cried, over the death of the plastic rose.
"Didya love 'im?" I said, and "do you take your coffee black?"
A public place is for the truly mad, therefore I carefully
  butter my bread.

*   *   *   *   *

Here are the potholes that yawn; here the yellow fruit
on a wooden stand. Winos dot night in a plume of fire,
devising reasons for the silver dress that pass them by.
Here is the double coin which knows no grief,
and the breast and the butt and the whiskey in a plastic cup.

These too I give you, old man, and the wallet holding a hint
  of ocean.
Consolation is in its circle, set in wet brown cowhide.
And here the snapshot of Berkeley campus, the flies
circling your crotch. Did I show you my cell at Bedlam,
where bunks are shaped like clocks?

*   *   *   *   *

Old man, I give you nothing, on this ordinary day.
I expose no new wounds to your ordinary eyes, staring
through sunlight's litter. And you, old man, with your boneless
  fish,
your collard greens and kool-aid, your dungarees rolled
above your cancerous, odorous knees,
would give the shift of seasons a bad name.
You'd drink vodka from the bottle
if your lips would say who.
You would cross your legs, if you knew what lay ahead.

57

But today is only yesterday in the rut of your favorite chair.

*   *   *   *   *

What's his name, this bureaucrat of placards. It's half-hidden
in gold, a friend of ornate trees, a stutter of acronyms
on a tobacco pouch. "Take a number please. In this public place.
I'm your host on this most sickly day."
And when you told him of the shrapnel, and of the missing leg,
and when I pressed his head against my purple heart,
we heard nothing but ourselves lewdly thrusting air.
We clung to the collars of our shirts, hearing only the silence
of wingtips and watercoolers, the ascension of dust amid
    daylight.

*   *   *   *   *

So what about the couple and the Don Q and Coke?
They are swaying in a room of thickening smoke.
And what about the death of the automobile?

Only silence, old workers, and untouched steel.

CYRANO

I've traveled so far on a White Castle and 6 cents,
on my way to a heart of darkness at a Melville Motel.
I can't give up the duffel bag of the insane.
I've tried.
I can't wrest control from the pilot who knows he'll crash.
I've tried, and I can't
do these things, then bargain with my own black heart.
I'm too much on my way, always,
to a chain of boxes wrapped specially for me,
with strings attached to this woman I met in Memphis.
I don't know her name.
I forget.
She sat astride a white van, and smoked
slender cigarettes. Perfume offended,
so she carried an amulet.
That's what I remember
about those bean sprout weekends
on my way to Calumet. Right
down yonder, and around some bend—where trees
shake their beady little stalks at passing men.
This place I too am bent on reaching, forever looking
for the whale's tooth, white as yonder slut, constantly probing
the cave that leaks, and searching
between its crack for the rock of precious answers,
the dry spot any gardener seeks. I've gone on
much too long. Moss on yonder trees turns
away, grows old, and one by one drops off.
I too have seen it all.
I don't regret.
I've enough for the toll at the quickest border,
which, I hear, is Calumet.

THE ROLE OF POETRY IN MY LIFE

Poetry serves for me as a crystalline form of discrimination. It is my nature, and sometimes my tragedy, to be passionate, to chart the thin but certain lines of Existence, to toy with the objects and ideas of intuition or emotion.

Personally, I am a recluse, a subjective observer of my self and other selves, and therefore, the only method available to me to express myself and to become a participant in the social activities around me is that of irration. Or, more precisely, the expression, indiscriminately, of the emotions and/or senses.

The world, to me, reflects many perceptions—so that even in order I am capable of perceiving disorder—and vice versa. As a poet, I attempt to make some sort of order out of the disorders I perceive around me.

Poetry, then, allows me the framework, the skeletal structure, the foundation on which I arrange the bits and pieces of disorder in my prodigal search for perfection. I do not aim for the nucleus of things, but I do seek their extremities, their variations, their innuendos, their shimmer in warm sunlight. It is my hope that by capturing these differences in my poetry, I can also capture individualities—and ultimately personalities, whether animate or inanimate.

Existentially, I am acutely aware of that common thread throughout Nature—which is "One-ness," or "The Way," or "Wu Wei." And it is precisely because of this awareness, or at least the Divinity of that common thread, which propels me toward the edges of existence, for it is only at the precipice, the limits of the landscape, that Things are most themselves—or in a sense capable of finding themselves, their true nature. But most importantly, it is also at the extreme, like a rubber band, that Things snap back to the heart, or center, or nucleus of Nature, and lose their individuality.

So it is only through poetry, the irrational, illogical, surreal elements of my poetry, that I am most capable of observing life at its limits, where Things are most themselves, naked under the discriminating aperture of my poetry.

Calvin Murry

BIOGRAPHY OF CALVIN MURRY

Calvin Murry is a native of Memphis, Tennessee, the youngest of ten children. His father was a Delta Blues guitarist, singer, tap dancer, magician, farmer, and trucker from Charleston, Mississippi. Before his death in a car accident in 1954, he methodically taught all his kids how to pick the guitar. Since Calvin was only 4 years old, and a left-hander, he was spared the traditional guitar lessons, but did learn to sketch and paint from his older brothers.

At the age of 17, Calvin left home and joined the Job Corps, in Morganfield, Kentucky, where he became the bantamweight boxing champ. He then went to Detroit, Michigan and attempted to turn professional—but was called back to Memphis to register for the draft. A month later he was sent to jail and convicted as an accessory to an armed robbery. He spent 6 years behind bars, was paroled—after surviving two poisonings, a stabbing, a fire and countless beatings and fights.

Three months while on parole, he was once again sent to prison, for 30 years. In sum, he has spent over 12 years behind bars. Calvin Murry is now 33 years old.

Mr. Murry has been published in over 30 U.S. periodicals, including JOINT CONFERENCE, SEZ Multi-Racial Jounal, OLD HICKORY REVIEW, DARK HORSE, GREENFIELD REVIEW NEWSLETTER, BLACKBERRY.

His reviews and critical articles have appeared in COMMERCIAL APPEAL's Mid-South Magazine, SOUTHERN EXPOSURE, GREENFIELD REVIEW NEWSLETTER, JOINT CONFERENCE, GRONDSWELL.

Mr. Murry is publisher and editor of GRONDSWELL Magazine, now in suspended publication, one of the few totally inmate owned and operated literary magazines devoted to prisoner writings.

Mr. Murry is a 3-time PEN Writing Awards for Prisoners winner, having won Honorable Mention in the Short Story category in 1979, 3rd place in the nonfiction category in 1978, and a creative writing correspondence course in 1977.

In 1980 Mr. Murry was one of 8 winners in the Eight Evenings of Poetry Contest, sponsored by St. Luke's Press and the Memphis Council of the Arts.

Mr. Murry has given readings throughout the South and Mid-West, and has appeared on numerous talk shows both on tv and radio. Recently, he was honored by Michigan's Poetry Resource Society to deliver a talk on Sterling Brown.